D1233354

SHOCK ZONE™
VILLAINS

PIRATES, SCOUNDRELS, AND SCALLYWAGS

MADELINE DONALDSON

Lerner Publications Company • Minneapolis

For Joe—my favorite pirate

Copyright © 2013 by
Lerner Publishing Group, Inc.

All rights reserved. International
copyright secured. No part of this book
may be reproduced, stored in a retrieval
system, or transmitted in any form or by any
means—electronic, mechanical, photocopying,
recording, or otherwise—without the prior
written permission of Lerner Publishing Group,
Inc., except for the inclusion of brief quotations in an
acknowledged review.

Lerner Publications Company
A division of Lerner Publishing Group, Inc.
241 First Avenue North
Minneapolis, MN 55401 U.S.A.

Website address: www.lernerbooks.com

Library of Congress Cataloging-in-Publication Data

Donaldson, Madeline.
    Pirates, scoundrels, and scallywags / by Madeline Donaldson.
      p. cm. — (ShockZone™—Villains)
    Includes index.
    ISBN 978–1–4677–0606–3 (lib. bdg. : alk. paper)
    1. Pirates—Juvenile literature. I. Title.
G535.D64 2013
910.4'5—dc23   2012018927

Manufactured in the United States of America
1 – CG – 12/31/12

TABLE OF CONTENTS

A PIRATE'S LIFE FOR YOU?

Avast ye! That means "stop and listen" in pirate speak. **Pirates had a lingo all their own.** But pirates weren't all alike. Some turned to piracy for money. Others had a grudge against the English or the French or the Spanish. They attacked them whenever they could. A few just liked fighting, no matter who was involved.

YAR, MATEY!
Pirates are also known as buccaneers and corsairs.

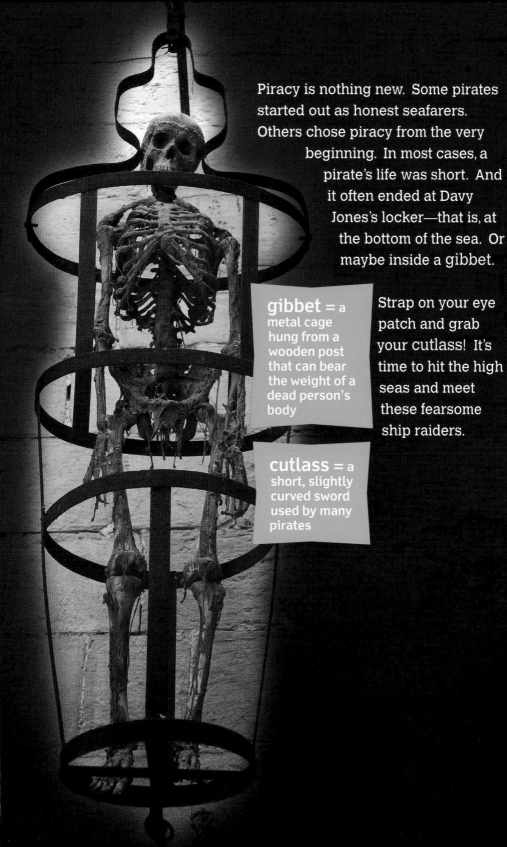

Piracy is nothing new. Some pirates started out as honest seafarers. Others chose piracy from the very beginning. In most cases, a pirate's life was short. And it often ended at Davy Jones's locker—that is, at the bottom of the sea. Or maybe inside a gibbet.

gibbet = a metal cage hung from a wooden post that can bear the weight of a dead person's body

Strap on your eye patch and grab your cutlass! It's time to hit the high seas and meet these fearsome ship raiders.

cutlass = a short, slightly curved sword used by many pirates

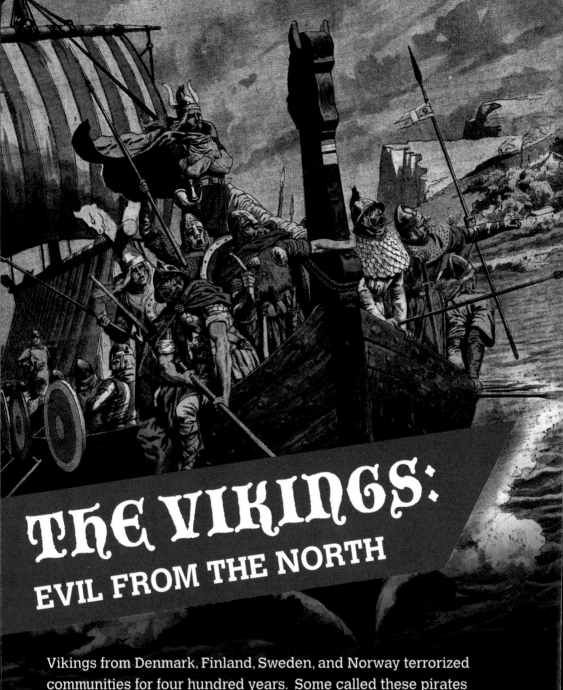

THE VIKINGS:
EVIL FROM THE NORTH

Vikings from Denmark, Finland, Sweden, and Norway terrorized communities for four hundred years. Some called these pirates the evil of the north. Viking raiders didn't fight much at sea. They mostly sailed their ships to shore, beached them, and attacked. Vikings were big and beefy. They carried heavy axes, broadswords, and wooden shields. They wore leather helmets. They tried to scare their victims by yelling loudly and swinging their weapons. They hacked away at townspeople and hauled away anything that looked valuable.

One of the Vikings' most famous targets was the abbey at Holy Isle in northeastern England. Abbeys are sacred places where monks live. The abbeys often hold valuable books and religious cups, crosses, and boxes covered in jewels. Monks usually have no way to defend an abbey. During the Holy Isle attack, Vikings slaughtered monks old and young. They ripped apart the abbey's sacred places. They looted its wealth.

Monks saved pages of the Lindisfarne Gospels from Viking raiders, but the book's jewel-encrusted cover was lost forever.

Vikings raided France, Ireland, eastern Europe, and the Middle East. Sometimes they used a hit-and-run style. Other times they set up camps that became towns. Some experts don't call these raiders pirates. But Vikings destroyed, butchered, burned, and looted. And those seem like pretty typical pirate things to do.

VIKING SPEAK
"Blast it! I mean to go a-Viking!" was what a Scandinavian might say when heading out to sea to plunder unsuspecting European towns.

plunder = to take valuable goods by force

7

THE BARBAROSSA BROTHERS: ARUJ AND HIZIR

Aruj and Hizir were born in a coastal village within the Ottoman Empire. Their dad was a successful potter. The empire stretched from North Africa to southeastern Europe and the Middle East. Both boys were good sailors who knew the Mediterranean Sea. In the late 1400s, Christian knights attacked one of their father's boats and took Aruj as a slave. He later gained his freedom. But he never forgot the insult.

In the early 1500s, Aruj met up with Hizir in North Africa. They began their pirate career with a focus on ships from Christian countries. One of their earliest successes was capturing a trading ship belonging to the pope—one of the richest Christians in the world! By this time, Aruj had a reddish beard. His look caused Europeans to nickname both the brothers Barbarossa (red-bearded).

By the early 1500s, Aruj and Hizir had built a fast pirate fleet. Within one month in 1512, the fleet captured twenty-three ships and lots of valuable cargo. The brothers were rich, powerful pirates of the Mediterranean. Spain, Italy, England, France, and the pope feared them. Aruj earned great respect as the pirate who ruled the North African coast. But he was killed in a battle in 1518.

Hizir took up where Aruj left off. For almost thirty more years, Hizir harassed European ships in the Mediterranean. The Ottoman ruler was grateful for Hizir's work. He made Hizir the governor-general of North Africa. Not bad for a couple of boys from a seaside pottery shop.

Ships commanded by the Holy Roman Empire were no match for the fleet of Hizir Barbarossa.

FRANÇOIS L'OLONNAIS:
FRENCH FANATIC

French-born François L'Olonnais (whose birth name was Jean David Nau) spent his early years as a Spanish slave. He grew up hating the Spaniards who ruled the Caribbean and Central America. He also didn't care much for the region's native peoples. Later, both groups had good reasons to steer clear of this angry French pirate.

Even among pirates, L'Olonnais was known as bloodthirsty. When he captured ships, he routinely killed entire crews. According to one report, he hacked a victim in two, pulled out the heart, bit it, and threw it back at a different prisoner. How's that for sending a message? He might have saved an unlucky crew member or two.

He'd brutalize them before setting them free to tell others of his cruelty. If native peoples were in the mix, he tortured and killed them as well.

His successful raids captured gold, silver, jewels, silks, and spices. They also attracted other pirates to join him. In 1667 L'Olonnais and several ships headed toward Maracaibo, a Spanish stronghold in modern

Don't want to have your heart cut out, bitten, and thrown at someone else? Be glad you never ran into L'Olonnais.

Venezuela. When they got to Maracaibo, the crew attacked. But the citizens had fled already. L'Olonnais's group hunted them down. They tortured the locals until they revealed where the town's wealth was hidden. The pirates left with a rich harvest.

Many of L'Olonnais's pirates sailed back to his hideout in Tortuga, off the coast of modern Haiti. But he wasn't satisfied. He wanted more treasure. He kept sailing in the area and ended up in northern Colombia. Native peoples captured him and gave him a brutal ending. While he was still alive, they tore his body into pieces and threw the parts into a fire pit. Some say they ate the broiled meat. No trace—or limb— of him survived.

L'Olonnais was always on the lookout to pick a fight with Spain.

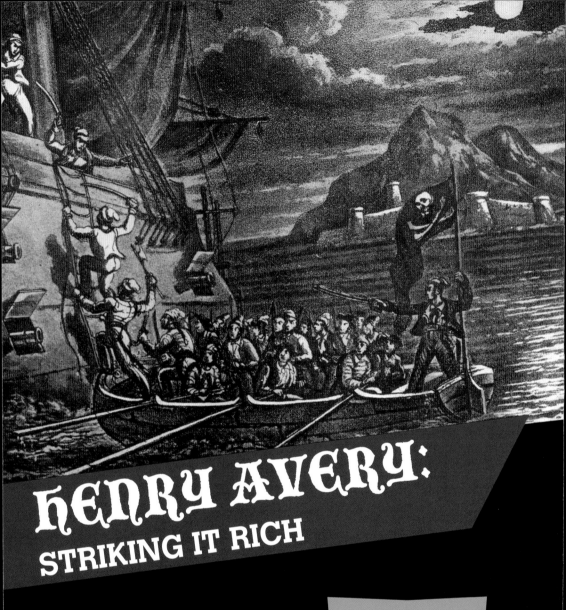

HENRY AVERY:
STRIKING IT RICH

Henry Avery may've been one of the few pirates who got to enjoy his loot. Some say he started out as a seaman in the British navy. From there, he worked on a privateer.

privateer = a privately owned ship given legal permission to attack the enemies of its owner's government

Henry's captain was a dirtball. So Henry took over the ship, turned pirate, and headed for the Arabian Sea near India. Henry knew ships with valuable cargo sailed back into the Arabian Sea after trade trips. He had to time his attack just right.

Avery captured a ship named *Ganj-i-Sawai*, which means "exceeding treasure." The loot made Avery the richest pirate in the world.

In 1695 he caught up with a big ship that belonged to the Indian emperor. It held goods worth perhaps $400 million in modern money. Henry focused on the gold, silver, and jewels. He and his crew tortured, killed, or threw overboard anyone who was in their way. Their behavior made them outlaws. Their riches made them legends.

With their massive loot, Henry and his crew headed to the Caribbean. They were looking for a safe place to hide. Maybe they could pay for a pardon from some easy-to-bribe official. They could live on a distant island, enjoying their riches. It didn't turn out that way.

The British government put a price on their heads. Some crew members went back to England. They were caught and hanged in

Was Henry Avery robbed while trying to sell his diamonds? Some think so.

1696. Henry stayed in hiding. He may have sailed back to England by way of Ireland. Some say he lived out his life quietly but in comfort. Others say he couldn't trade his diamonds and jewels into actual money and lived in poverty. No one really knows.

EDWARD TEACH:
FLAMING BEARD

Blackbeard—aka Edward Teach—was the most famous pirate known to ordinary folks. Blackbeard made sure people remembered him. He did, in fact, have a long black beard. Before an attack, he threaded his hairy locks with twine. He set the twine on a slow burn. So when a boat saw him coming, his beard was smoking. He shouted. He roared. He was one scary dude.

Blackbeard didn't always fight his victims. He preferred to scare them into surrendering. Often the moment they saw his flag, they gave up. Then his crew boarded their ships and took every bit of loot they could steal. Sometimes the take was grain or cloth or rum. Sometimes it was silver or gold.

His favorite place to hide was off the coast of North Carolina. The local British officials there became fed up with his activities.

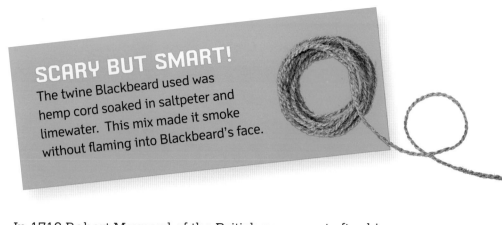

SCARY BUT SMART!
The twine Blackbeard used was hemp cord soaked in saltpeter and limewater. This mix made it smoke without flaming into Blackbeard's face.

In 1718 Robert Maynard of the British navy went after him. Blackbeard's ship attacked Maynard's. The pirate's crew thought they'd won. But the British hid. Maynard's men burst on deck, firing their pistols and swinging their swords. Blackbeard's men weren't prepared for the attack. Many lost their lives.

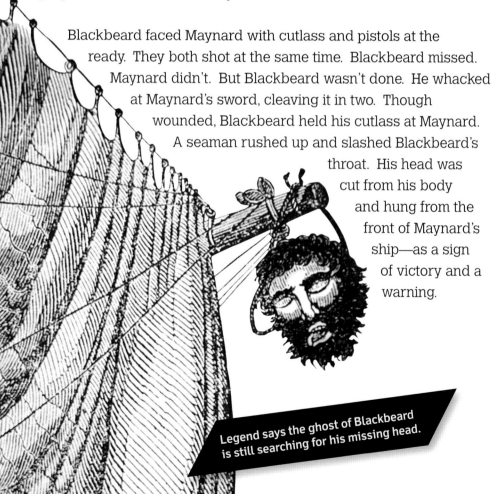

Blackbeard faced Maynard with cutlass and pistols at the ready. They both shot at the same time. Blackbeard missed. Maynard didn't. But Blackbeard wasn't done. He whacked at Maynard's sword, cleaving it in two. Though wounded, Blackbeard held his cutlass at Maynard. A seaman rushed up and slashed Blackbeard's throat. His head was cut from his body and hung from the front of Maynard's ship—as a sign of victory and a warning.

Legend says the ghost of Blackbeard is still searching for his missing head.

STEDE BONNET:
THROWING IT ALL AWAY

Stede Bonnet was a wealthy landowner in Barbados. He was educated, had a nice family, and rubbed elbows with the best of Barbadian society. So in the spring of 1717, when he sneaked out to play pirate, no one could explain why. Some suggested Bonnet had an "uneasy" mind. Others said he was escaping his crabby wife.

Bonnet bought a ship in secret and had it outfitted for piracy. He paid for guns to be put in and expanded the cargo space—for all the plunder he intended to find. Paying for these changes was unusual. Most pirates refitted a ship they stole rather than outfit one from scratch. Another oddity was his way of attracting a pirate crew. Bonnet had no seafaring skill. He needed skilled sailors. He offered steady wages instead of a share of what was stolen. Most of the crew that joined him was also inexperienced.

Even though Bonnet was often called the Gentleman Pirate, he still didn't escape the gallows.

Given Bonnet's lack of skills, he had surprising success. He first attacked ships along the Carolinian and Virginian coasts. Bonnet and his crew then met Blackbeard. Blackbeard agreed to join forces. But when he realized Bonnet didn't know how to sail, he took over Bonnet's ship. Bonnet spent time as the other pirate's prisoner.

Bonnet torched every ship he captured. Traders in the Carolinas grew tired of having pirates pillage and burn their ships. Soon the British navy was on the lookout. Bonnet had the bad luck to be among those the navy found. He and his crew were captured and put on trial. Bonnet tried to use his wealth and position as a way to get a pardon. But in November 1718, he was publicly hanged in Charleston, South Carolina.

pillage = to rob and destroy people's property

JACK & ANNE & MARY: FEARSOME THREESOME

Jack Rackham was a dud as a pirate. His targets were small boats. The stolen cargo wasn't much to brag about. But Jack got enough treasure to get by. He also got two women to sign on with him. One was his girlfriend, Anne Bonny. The other was a seafaring hearty named Mary Read.

Jack met Anne in 1719 in the Bahamas. She was married, but the pair sneaked off to sea. Anne was a wild woman. She dressed as a man during battle and wasn't shy about wielding her cutlass and guns and swords. While hunting small merchant ships, she and Jack captured a large vessel. Its crew included another woman disguised as a man. Mary was a bold, tough sailor who was used to shipboard life. She chose to join Jack's gang.

merchant ships = privately owned oceangoing boats that pick up and deliver cargo

In 1720 Jack and his crew stole a sloop, called the *William,* in the Bahamas. Using this boat, Jack's crew became famous for their ruthless fighting skills—especially Anne and Mary. The Bahamian governor was seriously annoyed.

sloop = a small but fast ship that could carry a lot of cargo

Jack's nickname was Calico Jack. He might not have made a great pirate, but his flag is still famous.

He sent privateers to take down the *William.* The hired guns attacked while Jack was plundering ships near Port Royal, Jamaica. Most of Jack's crew lay below deck, the worse for wear from a night of celebrating. On deck, the hired guns met only Anne and Mary. The women fought back savagely.

Jack and his entire crew were arrested, tried, and sentenced to death. Anne and Mary pleaded for mercy because both were pregnant. Jack's dead body was put on display near Port Royal to show what could happen to pirates. Mary died in prison the next year. No one knows for sure what Anne's fate was.

Mary Read (*left*) could duel as well as any man.

BARTHOLOMEW ROBERTS:
SMOOTH OPERATOR

Which real pirate matches the movie pirate Jack Sparrow? Many think he's modeled after Bartholomew Roberts. He was wildly successful. He was a smooth talker who had a way with women. Sound familiar?

But avast ye! He didn't start out as a pirate. In 1719 pirates attacked the merchant ship on which Roberts served. Whether he was forced on board or volunteered is unclear. But he proved to be a skilled seafarer and leader. The captain and his crew took notice. Six weeks later, the captain was killed during an attack. The crew elected Roberts to replace him.

Roberts easily took to piracy. Off the coast of Brazil, Roberts attacked a fleet of forty-two ships. The pirates came away with forty thousand gold coins and jewels. Soon after this success, a crew member double-crossed Roberts. So Roberts came up with a set of rules called articles. He made each crew member

Roberts's death shocked his crew.

swear by them. Each member had a vote in making decisions. Everyone would get an equal share of food and drink. Gambling was forbidden. Lights out was at eight o'clock. Women were not allowed on board. Stolen booty would be shared by the entire crew, from the captain to the lowest seaman.

The articles gained Roberts a loyal crew, including many African shipmates. They sailed up and down North America and along the Caribbean coast, claiming ships and their cargoes. Within a couple of years, Roberts had captured, looted, and destroyed more than four hundred ships. Some say his fleet single-handedly stopped the shipping business in these areas.

In April 1721, the fleet headed across the Atlantic to West Africa. A British navy vessel in the area attacked Roberts's ship in February 1722. A lucky spray of iron pellets hit Roberts in the throat. He died instantly. Members of his crew weighted down his body and threw it overboard so the British couldn't claim it.

Do you see a resemblance between Jack Sparrow *(above)* and Bartholomew Roberts?

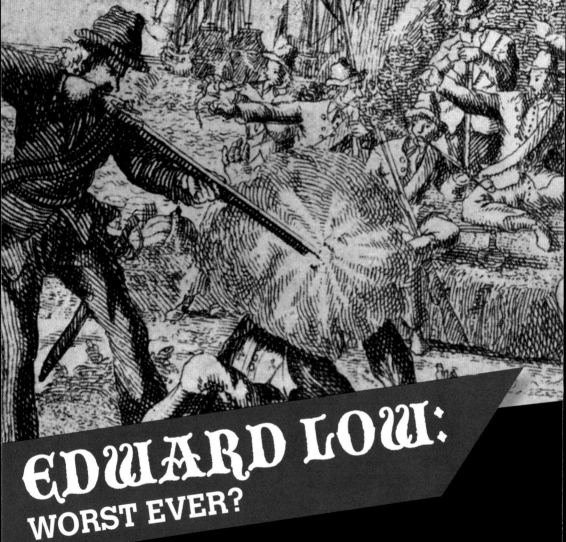

EDWARD LOW:
WORST EVER?

Edward Low was born poor in London, England, around 1690. He grew up big for his age and became a small-time thug. He moved on to gambling and burglary before heading to North America.

By 1722 he was in charge of his own pirate ship. He worked the sealanes of the American eastern coast. He also began to develop brutal tactics. One was to lace a victim's hands with twine and then set the twine on fire, burning the flesh down to the bone. Captured sailors were often chained and then beaten. Cutting off an ear or a nose tip with a cutlass was common. Low burned most ships after taking all the loot.

Edward Low burned most of the ships he captured.

One doomed captain kept Low from his loot by dropping the riches overboard. Outraged, Low sliced off the captain's lips. Then he broiled them and force-fed them to the captain's first mate. Low topped off this feat by killing the entire crew. Tactics like these scared future victims into surrendering without a fight.

In 1723 the British navy was hot on his trail. The navy managed to defeat Low's fleet. But Low and a small number of men escaped. By 1724 even Low's crew was fed up with his brutality. They threw him in a small boat and pushed him out to sea. He was picked up by a French merchant ship. But the crew knew who he was. The ship brought him to French-ruled Martinique. Some say the French hanged him. Others say he escaped.

The skeleton on Low's flag wasn't white. It was red—which meant he wouldn't take any prisoners.

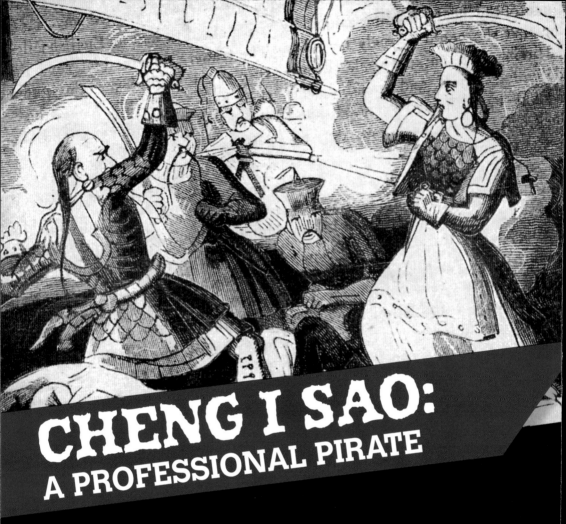

CHENG I SAO:
A PROFESSIONAL PIRATE

Maybe the most successful pirate ever—man or woman—operated far from the Caribbean Sea. In 1801 a smart, forceful woman named Shih Yang married Cheng I. Cheng was a pirate captain in the South China Sea. Together, they built a massive fleet. It numbered four hundred ships and seventy thousand sailors (some say fifteen hundred ships and eighty thousand sailors!). Cheng died in 1807, and Cheng I Sao (aka Shih Yang) took control of their fleet.

Cheng I Sao was a good organizer. She worked to expand her reach. Her pirates not only raided ships. They also demanded payment for kidnapped victims and for protection against being robbed—by Cheng's pirates! Captured seamen had the choice of joining her ranks or experiencing a long, slow death.

QUITE A CHARACTER

Cheng I Sao appears as the Asian pirate leader Mistress Ching in *At World's End*, the third Pirates of the Caribbean movie.

Like Bartholomew Roberts, Cheng had a set of pirate rules. Hers were stricter than Roberts's articles, though. Execution was one of the possible punishments for disobeying an order and for stealing or hiding plunder. Deserters lost their ears.

deserters = seamen who leave a ship without permission

Cheng retired from piracy by setting up a gambling house.

By 1810 Cheng's pirate fleet was as big as that of many nations. The Chinese government's navy took her on but lost. Without many options, the government offered her a pardon. Cheng was no slouch at bargaining. She agreed to stop her pirate activities. But she got to keep all the riches her fleet had stolen. She was not punished for piracy either. Cheng set up a successful gambling house in Guangzhou, where she died happy and rich.

MODERN PIRATES:
A RETURNING DANGER

Since 2000 some people from the East African nation of Somalia have taken to the high seas as pirates. Their country has no stable government. The people have to find their own ways of making a buck. However, Somali pirates have managed to get big guns to **scare people** in small boats, including people

Members of the Coast Guard were able to capture these pirates before anyone was hurt.

on vacation. They have charged massive fees for freeing hostages. Unlike pirates of old, they don't normally want more than ransom. They are not interested in building a pirate fleet. They seek short-term gains. But they are willing to murder their hostages.

At first, their activities didn't attract much attention. But over time, the frequency and nastiness of their work brought international attention. These days, the seafaring services of many nations are on the lookout for these pirates. Their successful work has weakened this outbreak of modern piracy. But the problem still exists.

Pirate Flags

Pirate captains used their flags as an easy-to-recognize calling card. As they got ready to attack, they'd raise their flag. They wanted their victims to know which pirate was about to capture them. Sometimes, upon seeing a flag, a ship would surrender without a fight.

Henry Avery's flag had a skull and crossbones—a standard pirate design, often called the Jolly Roger.

Blackbeard's showed a devil-horned skeleton holding an hourglass (a way of showing time running out) while sticking a spear into a red heart.

Bartholomew Roberts hated the people of Barbados and Martinique. His flag showed him with a foot on two skulls, one marked ABH and the other AMH. These stood for a Barbadian head and a Martiniquais head.

Jack Rackham was a bit more inventive. His skull had crossed cutlasses beneath it. (The Tampa Bay Buccaneers football team uses something similar as its flag but with a football under the chin of the skull.)

Tools of the Trade

Flintlocks

In the early 1700s, flintlocks were among the most common pirate guns. Portable and lightweight, several could be carried in holsters across a pirate's chest. The guns were fired when a wadded-up, easy-to-light package of gunpowder was placed in the gun and set on fire. But reloading wasn't so easy. Some pirates wore multiple loaded pistols. In a pinch, the guns' handles could be used as clubs.

Cutlasses

Cutlasses were the weapon of choice for pirates the world over. These short, thick swords were ideal for slashing and gouging. Most were curved. Some were straight. Cutlasses could just as easily cut through thick rope as a man's neck or thigh. They worked well in the tight spaces where shipboard fights often took place.

Pieces of Eight

Most British colonies didn't mint (make) coins. This was partly because not much gold or silver was mined locally at the time. Instead, British colonies used Spanish coins, called *reales*. Spain was a huge trader in the Caribbean and the Americas, so its coins were plentiful. Reales could easily be cut into eight parts. This is where the saying "pieces of eight" came from.

Grappling Hooks

These small hooks allowed pirates to grab hold of a victim ship's siding from a long distance. By pulling on the hook, pirates could haul the ship closer for boarding and pillaging. Game over!

Adventure on the High Seas
http://www.nationalgeographic.com/pirates/adventure.html
Kids can search for treasure and learn about pirates at this great site.

Farman, John. *The Short and Bloody History of Pirates.* Minneapolis: Millbrook Press, 2003. Quirky artwork gives readers an idea of how pirates really lived.

Fontes, Justine, and Ron Fontes. *Captured by Pirates.* Minneapolis: Graphic Universe, 2007. In this first title in the Twisted Journeys series, you control the action as you try to escape a band of pirates.

Get More Info about Pirates
http://www.babelgum.com/5004956/pirates-viking-pirates.html
This site has many documentaries on pirates throughout the ages.

International Talk like a Pirate Day
http://www.talklikeapirate.com/piratehome.html
This holiday is celebrated every year on September 19, and you can check out the website to learn about pirattitude.

Jacobs, Pat. *I Wonder Why Pirates Wore Earrings, and Other Questions about Piracy.* New York: Kingfisher, 2012. The question-and-answer format gives readers an easy way to browse information about pirates.

Krull, Kathleen. *Lives of the Pirates: Swashbucklers, Scoundrels (Neighbors Beware!).* New York: Harcourt, 2010. Krull takes readers through the long history of piracy.

Learn to Speak like a Pirate
http://www.syddware.com/cgi-bin/pirate.pl
This site translates regular English into pirate speak. Aaarr!

Lubber, William. *Pirateology.* Somerville, MA: Candlewick Press, 2006. This fun book follows the journey of Captain Lubber. Along the way, readers get a taste of pirate life and learn pirating skills.

Malam, John. *You Wouldn't Want to Be a Pirate's Prisoner!: Horrible Things You'd Rather Not Know.* Danbury, CT: Children's Press, 2002. The fun illustrations tell you exactly how it would feel to be captured by pirates.

Mathews, John. *Pirates.* New York: Atheneum, 2006. This book focuses on piracy in the Caribbean in the 1600s and the 1700s.

The Pirate Museum
http://thepiratemuseum.com/
This kid-friendly site goes with a pirate museum in Saint Augustine, Florida.

INDEX

LERNER
SOURCE

Expand learning beyond the printed book. Download free, complementary educational resources for this book from our website, www.lerneresource.com.

PHOTO ACKNOWLEDGMENTS

The images in this book are used with the permission of: © Paris Pierce/Alamy, p. 4; © Cahir Davitt/AWL Images/Getty Images, p. 5; © Leemage/Universal Images Group via Getty Images, p. 6; © Bridgeman Art Library, London/SuperStock, p. 7 (both); © Lebrecht Music and Arts Photo Library/Alamy, pp. 8, 11 (top), 12, 22, 24; © Universal History Archive/Universal Images Group/Getty Images, p. 9; © Roger-Viollet/Getty Images, pp. 10, 11 (bottom); © Peter Newark American Pictures/The Bridgeman Art Library, pp. 13 (top), 15 (bottom), 19 (bottom), 29 (second from bottom); © Mary Evans Picture Library/The Image Works, p. 13 (bottom); © Hulton Archive/Getty Images, pp. 14, 21 (top); © iStockphoto.com/Yuriy Chaban, p. 15 (top); The Granger Collection, New York, pp. 16, 17, 18; © Scope/Alamy, p. 19 (top); © British Library, London, Great Britain/HIP/Art Resource, NY, p. 20; Walt Disney/The Kobal Collection/Art Resource, NY, p. 21 (bottom); © Art Media, Great Britain/HIP/Art Resource, NY, p. 23 (top); © Todd Strand/Independent Picture Service, p. 23 (bottom); Walt Disney/The Kobal Collection/Vaughan, Stephen/Art Resource, NY, p. 25 (top); © Bettmann/CORBIS, pp. 25 (bottom), 28 (top and bottom); U.S. Navy photo by Mass Communication Specialist 2nd Class Jason R. Zalasky, p. 26; U.S. Navy photo by Mass Communications Specialist 1st Class Eric L. Beauregard, p. 26; © Topham/The Image Works, p. 28 (second from top and second from bottom); © The Board of Trustees of the Armouries, Leeds, England/HIP/Art Resource, NY, p. 29 (top); © Tria Giovan/CORBIS, p. 29 (second from top); © Dorling Kindersley/Getty Images, p. 29 (bottom).

Front cover: © SuperStock/SuperStock.

Main body text set in Calvert MT Std Regular 11/16.
Typeface provided by Monotype Typography.

J 910.45 DONALDSON
Donaldson, Madeline.
Pirates, scoundrels, and scallywags /
R2001118856 PALMETTO

ODC

Atlanta-Fulton Public Library